This Dinosaur

Kate McGough

AF605656

Look at the dinosaurs!

Pachycephalosaurus
(pak-ee-sef-ah-lo-sawr-us)

Parasaurolophus
(pa-ra-sawr-oh-loff-us)

Hypsilophodon
(hip-sih-lof-u-don)

Barosaurus
(ba-ro-sawr-us)

Gastonia
(gas-toe-nee-uh)

Ankylosaurus
(an-kie-loh-sawr-us)

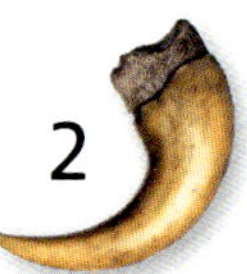

Stegosaurus
(steg-oh-sawr-us)

Velociraptor
(ve-loss-i-rap-tor)

Baryonyx
(bar-ee-on-iks)

Brachiosaurus
(brack-ee-oh-sawr-us)

Triceratops
(try-serra-tops)

Tyrannosaurus Rex
(tie-ran-oh-sawr-us rex)

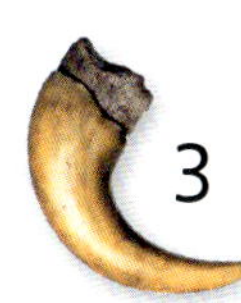

Horns

Look at this dinosaur.
This dinosaur has three horns on its head.

This dinosaur has a long horn on its head.

Claws

Look at this dinosaur.
This dinosaur has big claws
on its hands.

rip
shred

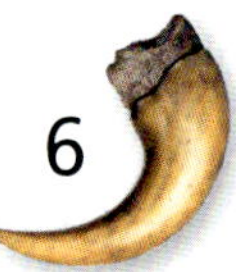

This dinosaur has big claws on its feet.

Tails

Look at this dinosaur. It has a club on its tail.

This dinosaur has a long, long, tail!

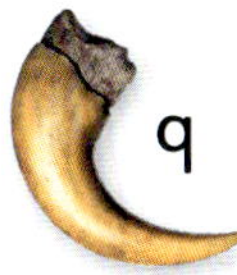

Spikes

This dinosaur has big spikes on its tail.

Swish

bang

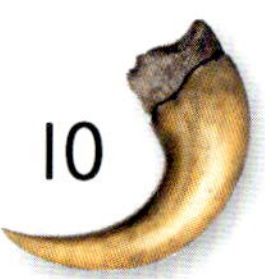

This dinosaur has lots of spikes on its back.

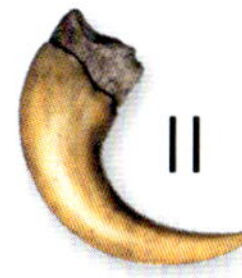

Necks

This dinosaur has a long neck.
It can eat the leaves in the trees.

chomp
chomp

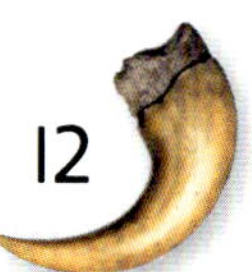

This dinosaur has a strong neck and head.

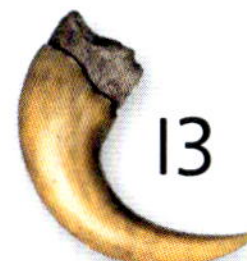

Teeth

Look at this dinosaur.
This dinosaur has **big** teeth!
It eats meat.

Run, dinosaur, run!

chomp chomp

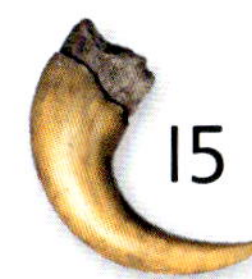

Picture Index